Hi. My name is Peter. My friends and I are students at East High School. We work after school. I work at a grocery store from three o'clock until five o'clock. I am a cashier. Here is where my friends work.

Jolene works at a video store on Fifteenth Street. Jolene always works on Friday, Saturday, and Sunday. She helps people find movies. She usually sees her friends in the store. Last week our classmates visited her at work. She talked to them about good movies.

Dean works in a sports store on Tenth Street. He usually works on Saturday and Sunday. On weekdays (Monday, Tuesday, Wednesday, Thursday, and Friday), Dean practices with his soccer team. At their game last week, Dean scored three goals. He kicked the ball, used his head, and ran very fast. He is a great athlete.

Colleen baby-sits two sisters after school. Jenny is five, and Pam is seven. They are very sweet. Colleen baby-sits them on Monday, Wednesday, and Friday afternoon. Yesterday she took them to the park. Then she read them stories. She also taught them new words.

My friend Juan works at a music store. He works on Tuesday and Thursday. He is handsome and nice. Girls always like Juan. Last week two girls shopped for music at his store. He talked to them for a long time.

Juan loves music. He plays the drums in a band on Friday and Saturday.

Gene likes to play guitar. He plays in Juan's band. They had a concert last month. Gene plays old songs, and he writes new ones. His music is beautiful.

Gene works at the music shop on Fourteenth Street. He always works on Thursday and Saturday. He teaches students how to play guitar.

Ana works in a coffee shop on Sunday and Monday. She makes coffee and tea. The coffee shop is near our school. Students often eat there. Ana sometimes sees her friends at work. She likes to talk to people. I saw her at the coffee shop yesterday.

Questions

A. Do you understand? Write your answers on a piece of paper.

   1. What days does Jolene work?

   2. Who plays in a band?

   3. What did Colleen do yesterday?

   4. What does Peter do after school?

B. Word Study

   1. Write six words that make the long *e* sound using ee.

      <u> week </u>   <u>   </u>   <u>   </u>

      <u>   </u>   <u>   </u>   <u>   </u>

   2. Write six words that make the long *e* sound using ea.

      <u> Dean </u>   <u>   </u>   <u>   </u>

      <u>   </u>   <u>   </u>   <u>   </u>

   3. Write six simple past tense verbs.

      <u> worked </u>   <u>   </u>   <u>   </u>

      <u>   </u>   <u>   </u>   <u>   </u>

C. Check Your Work

Compare your answers with your teacher's answers. Correct your mistakes.